AF244958

THE 12 SECRETS OF EXCEPTIONAL NONPROFIT LEADERS

THE KEY TRAITS NECESSARY TO DRIVE SOCIAL IMPACT

JAMES RUELL

© Copyright - James Ruell 2021 - All rights reserved.

The content contained within this book may not be reproduced, duplicated or transmitted without direct written permission from the author or the publisher.

Under no circumstances will any blame or legal responsibility be held against the publisher, or author, for any damages, reparation, or monetary loss due to the information contained within this book. Either directly or indirectly. You are responsible for your own choices, actions, and results.

Legal Notice:

This book is copyright protected. This book is only for personal use. You cannot amend, distribute, sell, use, quote or paraphrase any part, or the content within this book, without the consent of the author or publisher.

Disclaimer Notice:

Please note the information contained within this document is for educational and entertainment purposes only. All effort has been executed to present accurate, up to date, and reliable, complete information. No warranties of any kind are declared or implied. Readers acknowledge that the author is not engaging in the rendering of legal, financial, medical or professional advice. The content within this book has been derived from various sources. Please consult a licensed professional before attempting any techniques outlined in this book.

By reading this document, the reader agrees that under no circumstances is the author responsible for any losses, direct or indirect, which are incurred as a result of the use of the information contained within this document, including, but not limited to, — errors, omissions, or inaccuracies.

CONTENTS

"A leader is one who knows the way, goes the way, and shows the way."

— JOHN C. MAXWELL

Dear Reader,

If you're new to a leadership role at a nonprofit or are looking for a quick guide that will help you improve your skills and show you how to lead your organization better, you've got the right copy in your hands.

My name is James and I am the Vice Treasurer and Director of a small London charity serving disadvantaged young people. I've led the charity across various aspects; these have included monitoring finances, creating forecasts and projections, improving program sustainability, and assisting with strategic decision-making and recruitment. My endeavours alongside those of my colleagues have ensured that our charity has doubled in size in just a short span of time, won several high-profile grants, taken on new service contracts with government bodies, and built a robust management team.

My purpose in writing this quick guide is to share with you, my peers, the knowledge I've acquired over the years that I believe will be of tremendous use to leaders of small to mid-sized nonprofits. I aim to bring to you the right tools, practices and literature to help you grow in your roles, excel at your work and distinguish yourselves as fantastic leaders.

In my experience, some leaders running nonprofits stand out as being truly exceptional; they have magnetic personalities, are able to deliver on their promises, juggle multiple responsibilities and engage diverse stakeholders with such finesse and influence that they seem 'born to lead'.

HOW DO THEY DO IT ALL? WHAT MAKES SOME LEADERS GOOD AND OTHERS GREAT?

Based on my experience and observations of the most impactful nonprofits around the world, I humbly present to you **12 essential secrets** I've discovered of the leaders at their helms. These cover a broad range of key ideas on networking, oration, delegation, belief in a mission, futuristic thinking, nuances of management, measuring success, uniting stakeholders, building trust, staying on top of the money, building leadership capacity, and leading in times of uncertainty.

Whether you choose to read these secrets sequentially or jump right to the ones that you resonate with the most, I hope they inspire you in your journey to take yourself and your nonprofit to the next level, and help you maximize the impact made by your work upon the world.

Yours sincerely, James Ruell

HOW TO GET A FREE COPY OF THE ULTIMATE 4-WEEK FUNDRAISE WORKBOOK

Would you like a free copy of *The Ultimate 4-Week Fundraise Workbook*?

Get free and unlimited access to the below ebook and all of my future books by joining my Fan Base.

Scan with your camera to join!

---

12 SECRETS OF EXCEPTIONAL NONPROFIT LEADERS

#1: They **network**. A lot.

#2: They wear their **elevator pitch** on their sleeve

#3: They believe deeply in their **missions**

#4: They **don't try to do it all**

#5: They keep one eye on the **future**

#6: They stay on top of the **money**

#7: They **unite people** towards a common vision

#8: They don't just *manage*, they *lead*

#9: They are obsessive about **measuring impact**

#10: They invest in building **trust**

#11: They build **leadership capacity** in their organizations

#12: They view every crisis as an **opportunity**

#1: THEY NETWORK. A LOT.

If you've recently been appointed or promoted to lead a nonprofit, chances are your networking helped you get here. Guess what – you're only getting started.

The role of networking in the successful leadership of a nonprofit simply cannot be exaggerated. In a world that's more interconnected than ever before, you've got to be constantly communicating with the *right* people. The best nonprofit leaders (and leaders in general) understand this all too well; Dr. Misner, the founder of BNI, the world's leading referral organization reports that executives who find networking integral to their work spend an average of **6.5 hours per week** networking and win **half of their clients** from the time spent doing so.

> As the leader of your nonprofit, **how much time do you spend networking per week?**

It's likely that maximizing the social impact of your nonprofit is at the top of your priority list. In order to address the momentous challenges of climate change, social injustice, and poverty facing nonprofits in the 21st century, breaking down silos and building powerful cross-section collaborations with governments, corporations and other nonprofits can help you substantially scale up your impact. As corporations and consumers become more conscious and responsible, and corporate information becomes more transparent, companies are increasingly aligning their profits with a meaningful **purpose** and often looking to partner with nonprofits working towards a cause that resonates with them. Exploring tie-ups with corporations can thus be beneficial both to you and your allies.

If you're looking for evidence of how far networking can take you, look to the example of Habitat for Humanity – more specifically, Habitat for Humanity Egypt (HFHE). With a focus on building networks, HFHE collaborated with companies with know-how of local knowledge and requisite contacts to deliver impact at a larger scale, and succeeded in building, on average, **5 times** the number of houses annually compared to the typical Habitat for Humanity country program. So, while the best leaders do indeed understand that it is crucial to have their in-house systems, processes, and departments in place, they additionally leverage the power of networking to run the world's most prominent nonprofits and effect social change at unprecedented levels.

The good news? Professional platforms such as LinkedIn can now instantly connect you to a global audience of about 550 Million professionals. Everything from nonprofit training seminars to fundraising events are now being hosted virtually. Entire nonprofit teams are being built remotely with technology having made access to talent pools global. Communication has never been more seamless, and networking has never been easier.

#2: THEY WEAR THEIR ELEVATOR PITCH ON THEIR SLEEVE

As a leader, if you're going to be constantly networking, it follows that you need to be talking about your nonprofit in *the right way*. Assume that you meet a potential donor with no background of the kind of work your nonprofit does. Or that you come across an exceptionally bright young graduate who'd make an excellent employee. Are you able to convince them of the importance of your cause? Are you able to get them excited to get onboard and build engagement with you?

The best nonprofit leaders **live** their organization's mission. They wear their elevator pitch on their sleeve, their knowledge about everything remotely related to their nonprofit's cause is intimidating, and their enthusiasm is contagious.

> Are you able to clearly explain, in simple and direct language, to anyone you speak with, **what it is that your organization is truly about**?

Why is it important for you to have an elevator pitch for a nonprofit?

When was the last time you spoke to someone and completely bought into the idea, vision, product or service they were speaking of, and couldn't wait to be associated with it? Chances are, you remember very well. That is exactly why you need an excellent elevator pitch – you want to be **clear**, **distinctive**, and **memorable** when you introduce yourself and your nonprofit's work. You want to make a lasting first impression. You want to establish what makes you and your organization unique. You want to get the listener so excited that they can't wait to join your cause. And most importantly, you want to be able to do so in 20-30 seconds, or within the span of one elevator ride.

How can you refine your pitch?

Here are some important suggestions to help you pitch your nonprofit better to anyone you speak to, be it a donor, another nonprofit leader, or volunteer:

- **Don't assume** that the person you're speaking with has any prior background knowledge of your work
- Develop or **refine** your mission statement and clearly articulate what you stand for
- Be **succinct** in your conversations
- Provide **relatable** examples of the partnerships you've built or narrate impressive statistics of the **impact** you've made
- **Include an ask** or a call to action that is tailored to who you are addressing

Any time you find yourself wondering if you should include something in your pitch, pause and ask yourself, *"what's in it for the listener?"*

If you'd like to get your thinking cap on right away, here's a quick template for you to use.

An easy way to make a lasting impression in 20 seconds

My name is <YOUR NAME> and I'm the Executive Director of <NONPROFIT NAME> Our organization <WHAT THE NONPROFIT DOES> for <THE COMMUNITY YOU SERVE> that allows them to <YOUR VALUE-ADD> Unlike <OUR COMPETITION> we <WHAT MAKES YOU DIFFERENT>
I'd love to connect with you further by <CALL to ACTION>

#3: THEY BELIEVE DEEPLY IN THEIR MISSIONS

The best leaders in the world **truly believe** in what they do. They are intrinsically motivated by and deeply connected to their organization's mission, because of which they are successfully able to:

- Communicate within their organization and with external stakeholders with ease and influence
- Holistically guide strategy and decision-making across various stakeholders with the nonprofit's cause as the north star

- Be excellent leaders and motivate their teams, volunteers and collaborators

You're likely to have seen several instances in your personal or professional life wherein the best in a person is brought out because they are driven by a clear sense of purpose and are working in alignment with it. This is exactly what your nonprofit's mission statement can help you do. It is the reason your nonprofit exists, and the key purpose behind all your endeavours.

Think of some of the world's most renowned nonprofit organizations and it's likely that you'll see they have an impressive mission statement: **TED** - *Spread Ideas,* **Smithsonian** - *The increase and diffusion of knowledge,* **World Wildlife Fund** - *to conserve nature and reduce the most pressing threats to the diversity of life on Earth…*Do you see how powerful a mission statement can be?

What is the WHY of your nonprofit? **WHY does it exist?**

With the dawn of the 21st century, nonprofit organizations have evolved significantly, and leaders of all ages, backgrounds and ethnicities are championing causes with immense impact. While some nonprofits around the world are scaling up in their missions of poverty alleviation and housing for all, others are leveraging technology and communication to develop innovative models to elevate human life.

Leaders of nonprofits around the world in 2021 are championing social impact at impressive scales. **Nuru International** has empowered over 130,000 people to lift themselves out of extreme poverty. **Black Girl Ventures** is helping women of colour grow through entrepreneurship by enabling improved access to capital and human resources. **Ameelio** is building free communication technology to help connect incarcerated people with their families and with necessary resources, services and learning tools, enabling the creation of a 'humane and rehabilitative justice system'. **The Global Sunrise Project**, founded by a Gen Z nonprofit leader, is using social media to educate and encourage youth to make a positive impact in their communities.

As the leader of a nonprofit in the 21st century, how are you leveraging technology, communication tools, and capital and human resources to maximize the impact of your organization's cause?

#4: THEY DON'T TRY TO DO IT ALL

"No man will make a great leader who wants to do it all himself, or to get all the credit for doing it."

— ADREW CARNEGIE

You may be familiar with the popular quote by Anthea Turner: *"The first rule of management is delegation."* Leaders at the helms of the world's best organizations, whether large or small, understand and implement this; they don't try to do it all by themselves, because they know they simply can't.

To unleash your leadership potential to its fullest and to be able to deliver on your responsibilities to the best of your capacity, follow these key rules recommended by other leaders.

Focus on doing what *only you can do*

There's one thing that Tim Cook and Jeff Bezos have in common in their leadership philosophy, as stated by technology media reporter Mr. Aten; both these leaders focus on dealing with issues that **only they can deal**

with, while refraining from micromanagement. They trust their teams completely with their responsibilities. Known as the "only you" principle, this practice suggests that leaders in charge of complex institutions and organizations often keep on top of their game through empowerment and delegation, which allows them to focus on the activities that absolutely require their attention.

Hire the best talent and trust your team

The best nonprofit leaders understand that an organization can only be as good as the people it comprises of. They scout for, recruit, empower and coach **the best talent.** Subsequently, they refrain from telling them what to do and instead outline high-level responsibilities clearly, articulate expectations well, encourage constant communication, and most importantly, truly **listen** to their employees.

Many leaders are initially afraid of delegation. However, remember that if you're a good leader/manager, you're coaching your employees well and constantly developing their managerial capacity (all of which you should be doing), you will likely find that **nothing** goes wrong when you leave things up to your them.

Track your time consciously and improve your efficiency

An article by the Harvard Business Review (HBR) cites that, on average, ~11% of a CEO's work time is spent on routine activities. Revisiting your calendar to spot out tasks that do not truly require your attention as a leader, identifying sessions or meetings with duplication in takeaways and decision-making or any other time-consuming processes that can easily be delegated or streamlined can help you free up your time. The study reports that on average, CEOs spend ~70% of their time within their organizations and ~30% with external stakeholders including collaborators, communities, clients, advisors, vendors, PR agencies, board of directors and other people.

As a leader, the more efficiently you manage your time within your organization, the more time you're able to spend in expanding your reach to enhance the change your nonprofit can make in the world. Here are some tips from time-management practices from global leaders and industry titans to help you maximize your efficiency: **Richard Branson** of the Virgin Group wakes up at 5 am to work out. Businessman, philanthropist and politician **Marcus Lemonis** makes a list of 5 items to 'knock out' and get done each day, no matter what. **Arianna Huffington** of The Huffington Post deliberately 'pauses' or breaks for lunch. Fitness entrepreneur **Tracy Anderson** maintains several little 'idea' notebooks to keep track of her thoughts.

What are the things that **only you can do** at your organization?

How completely do you trust your teams and how much do you really listen to them?

How consciously do you keep track of your time? What tools do you use to enhance your productivity?

#5: THEY KEEP ONE EYE ON THE FUTURE

If the pandemic of 2020 has taught us anything, it is that leaders who are prepared to embrace change and steer their organizations through turbulent times will emerge as winners. Nonprofits need to be adaptable and innovative, and the best leaders always tend to keep one eye on the future. The world is still reeling under uncertainty across multiple industries – as we come out onto the other side into a 'new normal,' you must prepare to enter a **new world of nonprofits**.

What does the future of nonprofits look like?

Statistics show that due to the pandemic, global food insecurity has risen substantially and close to 70 million people have been pushed back into poverty; amidst these global challenges, nonprofits will need to **improve their outreach** and increase the support towards their communities. As per a Salesforce study, the nonprofit sector is expected to evolve substantially in the near term; nonprofits will need to **leverage data-driven analytics** and **digital branding** for better connectivity with communities and donors. Additionally, **data management tools** are expected to become integral in monitoring processes, tracking funds and managing nonprofits.

Here are some fantastic examples of how some nonprofits around the world are stepping into the future:

- In anticipation of a more honest and collaborative relationship between donors and nonprofits, the Malala Foundation uses technology to keep track of their donor interactions through their journey with their foundation, in an attempt to **personalize communications and relationships** with each donor.

- In order to improve using **community feedback**, Open Door Legal uses a knowledge database to collate legal cases for marginalized communities.
- Upaya hosted a fundraising round through a **virtual event** in replacement of its black-tie gala in support of its cause of helping scale-up businesses for people living in poverty.

As a leader, **how future-ready** are you building your nonprofit to be?

Revisit your key responsibilities

As you get ready to stay on top of the new opportunities that the future brings you, don't forget that each of your core functions as a leader will also evolve and that you need to be refining your systems and processes across each of these. **Financial management** will improve in speed and accuracy with the right tools; fundraising will go digital, you'll need to update **communications** for better **governance**, manage your **remote teams** virtually and invest in building **trust** for your community and donors by leveraging **digital branding**.

#6: THEY STAY ON TOP OF THE MONEY

If you're running a for-profit corporation, the customer is the king and determines financial performance and organizational growth. As you're aware, it gets a little more complicated in the world of nonprofits. Leaders need to be able to articulate the nonprofit's programs/needs for funding, and to be able to develop sources of funding that correspond well with those requirements, whether these are government endowments, individual contributions, corporate donations or foundation grants.

Leverage digital communication

Whether your approach to fundraising is more 'mass-market' or is dependent on a few key donor relationships, you don't want to overlook the value of building trust, and the role that having a credible digital brand can play in your funding. Is your **social media** page representative of your nonprofit's mission, does it resonate with your community and donors, and does it inspire trust? Is your **website** professionally made with clear contact information enlisted? Do you and other senior executives stay in touch with key stakeholders via **email correspondence** and **newsletters** beyond your day-to-day emails? Would more **advertising** or

PR activities help your cause with visibility? Are your teams on top of **virtual events** or galas that might help expand your organization?

Collaborate for higher impact

An HBR study mentions that about 80% of millennials today cite that it is more important for them to positively impact the world than it is to gain professional recognition. This necessitates that for-profit corporations begin to take the **purpose** of what they do more and more seriously, and look beyond profits if they genuinely want their customers' loyalty. They want to increasingly affect positive social change and can do so by sharing their resources and partnering with nonprofits to scale up social impact substantially, thus creating a win-win situation.

Get better at engaging your donors

There are various sources of funding, but to a large extent, it is the relationships between a nonprofit's leader and its donors as well as the resonance of the cause of the nonprofit with the donors that will determine funding. Try to get regular feedback from your donors to improve your organization's efforts. Try to get their opinions by cultivating better relationships. And don't overlook the importance of keeping them apprised by quantifying and communicating the impact of the work you're doing with their funding where relevant.

Is your nonprofit putting its **best foot forward** in terms of its visibility and credibility to attract suitable donors?

Are you thinking out of the box when it comes to fundraising and **cross-sector collaborations**?

#7: THEY UNITE PEOPLE TOWARDS A SHARED VISION

What draws you to professionals you believe to be excellent leaders? Chances are, it's their ability to visualize and inspire you towards the future with a magnetism that pulls you in. This is precisely what makes good leaders **great** – they can unite people with different agendas, whether from within various parts of an organization or outside it. Having a clear vision and articulating this for others allows a leader to inspire action, provide a clear direction, bring various teams together, and provide a sense of purpose.

From a more strategic point of view, having a distinct vision for your nonprofit will also allow you to clarify your scope of work in alignment with your organization's values and help you determine what *not* to do – which is often imperative for nonprofits as they work with limited resources.

"The essence of strategy is choosing what NOT to do"

— MICHAEL PORTER

The best leaders are also **masters of engagement**. You must be able to engage your employees well to retain the best talent. You'll need to inspire and engage volunteers so that they find meaning in their efforts and contributions. You want to be great at engaging your community and your board, and as you're already aware, engaging donors well is crucial to the success of your nonprofit.

How do you better engage these diverse stakeholders, each with their own mindsets and agendas?

Here are a few suggestions to get you started:

- Create a positive work environment that inspires a diverse workforce
- Invest in coaching and developing leadership capabilities in your team to help them grow
- Be transparent about your nonprofit's goals and values to provide a clear sense of direction
- Entrust volunteers with important responsibilities to ensure enthusiastic participation
- Promote brand advocacy by your volunteers and employees
- Maintain healthy communication and remain accessible
- Lay out clear expectations and instructions
- Provide a sense of community and inclusivity within your organization
- Invest in developing collaborations with other nonprofits
- Encourage your teams to build visibility in the community by attending events

What are your go-to methods to build better engagement within and around your nonprofit?

#8: THEY DON'T JUST *MANAGE*; THEY *LEAD*.

"Management is doing things right; leadership is doing the right things"

— PETER DRUCKER

In running your nonprofit, you may be an excellent manager and not necessarily a good leader. It could also be the other way around – you could have great leadership traits but not managerial acumen. Naturally, every organization needs both to thrive, but to ensure this, you'll need first to take a quick step back and understand what makes leadership and management different.

Leading and managing – what's the difference?

Leaders are essentially concerned with **setting a vision** and charting out a course for their cause or mission. In contrast, managers are essentially concerned with the **successful administration** of their organization's activities and operations to achieve specific goals. In other words, leaders concern themselves with *the future* and with *the changes* required to get there, whereas managers concern themselves with *execution in the present* by means of *systems and processes* of the organization. To shape an exceptional future for your nonprofit, you need to learn how to wear both hats adeptly; that of a leader and that of a manager.

What are some characteristics of the best nonprofit leaders?

Chances are, you've come across some charismatic leaders in your professional life – people who seem to fit the role of a leader with extraordinary ease. There are, however, some specific and common characteristics that make these excellent leaders stand out, and you can work on these skills to hone your leadership abilities.

Take a quick look at this list of traits of good leaders – how many of these are you confident in, and which ones do you need to spend more time on for yourself?

- They lead with **purpose**. In a world becoming more and more conscious, leadership and organizations with clarity of purpose stand to win

- They're passionate about and **dedicated** to their cause
- They are **inspiring** and their belief in their vision is contagious
- They are excellent orators and communicators
- They believe in and **truly listen** to their teams
- They know how to work with limited resources and **navigate uncertainties** without getting overwhelmed
- They are **authentic** and are not afraid to get **personal**
- They don't operate based on assumptions and instead invest in acquiring real **knowledge**
- They are **trustworthy** and have earned their reputation over time through their actions, thoughts, decisions and relationships

What sets YOU apart as a leader? How are you honing your leadership skills?

#9: THEY ARE OBSESSIVE ABOUT MEASURING IMPACT

As you envision the strategic direction of your nonprofit, you're likely to repeatedly ponder the answer to the question, "what is the problem that we are trying to solve?" While you have an idea of this based on your nonprofit's vision, as a leader, you want to **define** the desired impact you aim to make, **articulate** this impact in quantifiable or objective terms, and **measure** these results.

Defining impact and subsequently measuring it helps you and your nonprofit gain credibility. As a leader, it enables you to improve the quality of the conversations you have with all stakeholders regarding your nonprofit's activities. It allows you to develop more significant relationships, attract more funding, gain the attention of the right potential collaborators, and even recruit better talent.

As you set out to measure the success of your nonprofit's endeavors, here are some questions to help you brainstorm with your team:

- What are the exact results you will hold yourself accountable for?
- How are you going to achieve these results?
- What resources do you need? How do you best plan for success?
- How do you best use your existing resources and better develop your capabilities as a nonprofit?

Do you see how having this sort of clarity in direction and target goals can help you guide your nonprofit better? If you're wondering what the next step is in measuring success, the answer lies in **data**. Besides tracking financial data that help illustrate the achievements of your organization's projects or programs, here are some guidelines from the consulting firm McKinsey to help you **correctly measure what matters**:

- Track data points that prove your nonprofit is executing/realizing its mission
- Track data points that help you monitor how your resources are being used
- Track data that illustrate the productivity of your teams
- Track fundraising data
- Track data on community engagement and scale
- Track data on various programs being implemented at your organization

How is desired impact defined at your nonprofit? **How do you measure success?** What data do you track?

#10: THEY INVEST IN BUILDING TRUST

You might wonder why you need to build a 'brand' around your nonprofit. While it will naturally help you with visibility to scale up, another important reason for establishing a brand is to inspire **trust**. With several nonprofits everywhere, the best nonprofit leaders understand the role of the brand, and invest in building awareness and credibility. Furthermore, a well-recognized nonprofit brand can help aid fundraising, act as a medium to express an organization's values and culture, and provide a sense of identity and unity.

> How visible is your brand? How well do your
> teams and community resonate with your
> brand's values?

In the context of brand-building, the most powerful tool at your disposal is social media. Social media can help you and your nonprofit in several ways:

- You can build general reach and visibility without incurring significant expenses
- You can organically reach/be discovered by potential stakeholders with an affinity for your cause

- You can conduct quick polls and surveys to gauge community response, donor opinions, and so on
- You can use social media channels to build and manage relationships
- You can express your organization's values and convey your impact by leveraging various mediums of storytelling such as tweets, images, or videos

If you're convinced of the advantages of investing time and resources to leverage social media platforms, the next step is to develop your brand strategy. Some suggestions to help you develop this include: deliberating upon your **uniqueness**, narrowing down on your **target audience**/community, revamping your **website**, **differentiating** yourself, communicating **relatability**, **personalization** for better relationship management, and **thought leadership** amongst others.

"If people believe they share values with a company, they will stay loyal to the brand"

— HOWARD SCHULTZ

#11: THEY BUILD LEADERSHIP CAPACITY IN THEIR ORGANIZATIONS

The best leaders understand that they can't build an A-level organization with a B-team. You want to **attract** and **retain** the best talent and provide them with the resources they need to do their best work. The best leaders also understand the necessity of 'capacity building,' or investing in building a cadre of leaders for the long-term sustainability of their nonprofit.

An HBR article cites that in the nonprofit sector, on average, only 30% of open high-level leadership positions are filled by internal candidates, as compared to 60% in the for-profit sector. As a leader at a nonprofit – do you see how you have your work cut out? As an executive director, mentoring those under your wing to be future leaders is a core responsibility for ensuring your organization's health and longevity. Further, about half the respondents surveyed in a study for employees leaving nonprofits mentioned a lack of professional growth and opportunities as their reason for their exit. Research shows that a significant 70% of learning and professional development in employees occurs through carefully chosen 'stretch' assignments provided by managers instead of only 10% of the learning that occurs through 'formal training.'

Are your employees happy with the growth prospects at your organization? Do they feel fulfilled and find meaning in their work? Are they being provided with enough challenges? Retaining good talent falls to you as the leader, and you want to ensure your managers are doing their best to nurture their respective teams.

"Before you are a leader, success is all about growing yourself. When you become a leader, success is all about growing others."

— JACK WELCH

The most efficient capacity-building process at organizations encompasses a threefold approach: improving workplace infrastructure, improving management and governance via the board and senior executives, and investing in the shaping of employees to be future managers and leaders. Investing in capacity building today will help you take your nonprofit to the next level of its growth in the future. While for-profit organizations generally take capacity building very seriously from both a future-growth mindset and a risk-alleviation mindset, nonprofits are yet to catch up.

If you're looking for suggestions on improving engagement and cultivating an atmosphere of growth at your organization, here are a few practices you can implement:

- Provide sufficient challenges and opportunities to your teams
- Outline mentorship programs with your managers
- Entrust your managers with more and more responsibilities
- Create a culture of continuous feedback
- Encourage all team members to speak up and ensure they know that their contributions are valued
- Invest in upskilling programs
- Involve your board members to share opinions on future growth
- Encourage group learning activities

Successful capacity building and establishing systems for coaching the next round of leaders at your organization will help ensure a strong foundation for your nonprofit and its mission in the years to come.

#12: THEY VIEW EVERY CRISIS AS AN OPPORTUNITY

"A leader takes people where they want to go. A great leader takes people where they don't necessarily want to go, but ought to be."

— ROSALYNN CARTER

The global pandemic has brought significant changes, some temporary and others permanent. It has underscored the need for agility, adaptability, coordination, collaboration, and technological prowess for corporations and nonprofits. The best leaders view crises as opportunities – opportunities to **pivot**, **reinvent**, **accelerate**, and **compete**. To successfully lead their nonprofit through uncertain times, they understand and implement two key themes: adapting to the new world without losing track of organizational fundamentals and values.

Embracing technology and adapting to the new world

Engagement of all stakeholders is now largely possible virtually, employing communication tools that have become ubiquitous. Whether it is your employees, volunteers, donors, community representatives, or even other nonprofit members, virtual meetings and events can help you stay on top of your activities. In many ways, a hybrid, if not wholly virtual model of engagement, is increasingly becoming the norm.

Digital presence can help you promote your nonprofit, reinforce your mission, connect with others with similar ideologies, reach out to donors, use crowdsourcing, develop popular campaigns for support for your cause, and communicate values via engaging media.

Looking for innovative ways to stand out online? The charity 'Water' hosted a Google Hangout fundraiser event, wherein speakers presented Q&A sessions and seats were available for purchase. New York based animal rescue shelter 'Social Tees Animal Rescue' created Tinder profiles for dogs to match potential owners. 'WATERisLIFE' used the hashtag '#firstworldproblems' to build visibility for a video showcasing people in dire living conditions, generating awareness for their cause.

How is your nonprofit shaping its digital presence? Are you using any innovative methods to stand out online?

Not losing sight of the fundamentals

As you reimagine your organization for the new age, you want to quickly revisit your duties as a leader and the fundamentals of why your organization exists. Remember that the focus of your endeavors should be to **maximize social impact** – so keep on top of who you serve and what difference you are trying to make in the world. You want to ensure your organization is a **wonderful place to work** and that your teams find **purpose** in their work. And last but not least, don't forget to keep on top of **money matters**.

Equipped with these 12 secrets, you're now on your way to unlock your leadership potential and take your nonprofit to the next level.

I hope this quick guide has brought you a lot more confidence and inspiration for your journey. Please leave a review if you enjoyed this book.

If you'd like further advice, content, tools, and support on the various nuances of leading and running a nonprofit, I invite you to join a network of like-minded peers on our Facebook community page *Nonprofit Leaders Community* by clicking here. Many people are already getting huge benefits from the community!

ALSO BY JAMES RUELL

Check out my other book - available on Amazon and Audible

Winning Grants: How to Write Winning Grant Proposals That Will Get You Funding for Your Nonprofit

BIBLIOGRAPHY

Adam, G. (2021, April 20). *32 Nonprofit Leaders Who Will Impact the World in 2021*. Causeartist - Social Entrepreneurship | Social Impact News. https://causeartist.com/nonprofit-leaders-who-will-impact-the-world-2021/

Bradach, J. L., Tierney, T. J., & Stone, N. (2014a, August 1). *Delivering on the Promise of Nonprofits*. Harvard Business Review. https://hbr.org/2008/12/delivering-on-the-promise-of-nonprofits

Elkins, K. (2017, February 17). *14 time-management tricks from Richard Branson and other successful people*. CNBC. https://www.cnbc.com/2017/02/17/time-management-tricks-from-richard-branson-other-successful-people.html

Gauss, A. (2019, February 26). *5 Smart Brand Strategies for Nonprofits*. Classy. https://www.classy.org/blog/5-smart-brand-strategies-nonprofits/

Gavin, M. (2019, October 31). *Leadership vs. Management: What's the Difference? | HBS Online*. Business Insights - Blog. https://online.hbs.edu/blog/post/leadership-vs-management

Lake, L. (2019, June 25). *Learn About the Benefits Non-Profits Gain from Social Media Marketing*. The Balance Small Business. https://www.thebalancesmb.com/social-media-marketing-benefits-for-non-profits-2295820

Landles-Cobb, L., Kramer, K., & Smith Milway, K. (2016, January 7). *Nonprofits Can't Keep Ignoring Talent Development*. Harvard Business Review. https://hbr.org/2015/12/nonprofits-cant-keep-ignoring-talent-development

Marciano, J. W. S. (2008). *The Networked Nonprofit (SSIR)*. Stanford Social Innovation Review. https://ssir.org/articles/entry/the_networked_nonprofit

Marlin Communications. (2020, October 2). *Top 6 Examples of*

Nonprofits making effective use of digital technology. Marlin Communications. https://marlincommunications.com/blog/top-6-examples-of-not-for-profit-organisations/

Misner, I. (2020, December 23). *How Much Time Should You Spend Networking?* BNI. https://www.bni.com/the-latest/blog-news/how-much-time-should-you-spend-networking

Myatt, M. (2017, March 17). *10 Communication Secrets Of Great Leaders.* Forbes. https://www.forbes.com/sites/mikemyatt/2012/04/04/10-communication-secrets-of-great-leaders/?sh=8866b8522fe9

Porter, M. E., & Nohria, N. (2021, February 13). *How CEOs Manage Time.* Harvard Business Review. https://hbr.org/2018/07/how-ceos-manage-time

Quantum Workplace. (2016). *Engaging Nonprofit Employees.* https://cdn2.hubspot.net/hubfs/99128/Website/Resources/PDFs/Engaging-Nonprofit-Employees-Industry-Report.pdf

Ragones, D. (2020a, December 15). *10 Nonprofits Using Tech to Build Resilience.* Salesforce.Org. https://www.salesforce.org/blog/10-nonprofits-using-tech-for-good/

Ragones, D. (2020b, December 30). *4 Ways Nonprofits Will Evolve in 2021.* Salesforce.Org. https://www.salesforce.org/blog/nonprofit-sector-evolve-2021/

Sawhill, J., & Williamson, D. (2020, December 4). *Measuring what matters in nonprofits.* McKinsey & Company. https://www.mckinsey.com/industries/public-and-social-sector/our-insights/measuring-what-matters-in-nonprofits#

Shepard, J. W. (2014, May 14). *Leadership Development: Five Things All Nonprofits Should Know (SSIR).* Stanford Social Innovation Review. https://ssir.org/articles/entry/five_nonprofit_leadership_development_facts

Steimle, J. (2014, March 14). *10 LinkedIn Fast Facts For Thought Leaders.* LinkedIn. https://www.linkedin.com/pulse/10-linkedin-fast-facts-thought-leaders-josh-steimle/

Stone, N. K. C. (2012). *The Role of Brand in the Nonprofit Sector (SSIR).* Stanford Social Innovation Review. https://ssir.org/articles/entry/the_role_of_brand_in_the_nonprofit_sector

Varga, J. (2021, March 7). *Tim Cook and Jeff Bezos share a management principle that has driven their success.* Express.Co.Uk.https://www.express.co.uk/life-style/science-technology/1406606/tim-cook-jeff-bezos-apple-amazon-netflix-management-principle-technology-ont

www.ingramcontent.com/pod-product-compliance
Lightning Source LLC
Chambersburg PA
CBHW032248070726

47590CB00017B/3059